THE
LOUISIANA
PURCHASE AND
WESTWARD
EXPANSION

THE
LOUISIANA
PURCHASE AND
WESTWARD
EXPANSION

EDITED BY
JEREMY KLAR

Britannica
Educational Publishing

IN ASSOCIATION WITH

ROSEN
EDUCATIONAL SERVICES

Published in 2016 by Britannica Educational Publishing (a trademark of Encyclopædia Britannica, Inc.) in association with The Rosen Publishing Group, Inc.
29 East 21st Street, New York, NY 10010

Distributed exclusively by Rosen Publishing.
To see additional Britannica Educational Publishing titles, go to rosenpublishing.com.

First Edition

Britannica Educational Publishing
J.E. Luebering: Director, Core Reference Group
Anthony L. Green: Editor, Compton's by Britannica

Rosen Publishing
Jeremy Klar: Editor
Nelson Sá: Art Director
Michael Moy: Designer
Cindy Reiman: Photography Manager

Cataloging-in-Publication Data

The Louisiana Purchase and westward expansion / edited by Jeremy Klar. — First edition.
     pages cm. — (Early American history)
 Includes bibliographical references and index.
 ISBN 978-1-68048-271-3 (library bound : alk. paper)
 1. Louisiana Purchase—Juvenile literature. 2. West (U.S.)—History—To 1848—Juvenile literature. 3. West (U.S.)—Discovery and exploration—Juvenile literature. 4. United States—Territorial expansio—Juvenile literature. I. Klar, Jeremy.
 F351.L68 2016
 973.4'6—dc23

2015017784

Manufactured in the United States of America.

Photo Credits: Cover, p. 3 Hulton Archive/Getty Images; p. 7 Library of Congress, Washington, D.C. (digital id: ppmsca 09855); p. 11 Classic Vision/age fotostock/SuperStock; pp. 13, 32-33, 41, 51, 58-59, 67 Encyclopaedia Britannica, Inc.; pp. 14-15, 30-31, 46 MPI/Archive Photos/Getty Images; pp. 18-19 Library of Congress Geography and Map Division; pp. 20-21, 49, 65 Library of Congress Prints and Photographs Division; pp. 22-23 Everett Collection/SuperStock; p. 27 Courtesy National Gallery of Art, Washington, D.C., Gift of Thomas Jefferson Coolidge IV in memory of his great- grandfather, Thomas Jefferson Coolidge, his grandfather, Thomas Jefferson Coolidge II, and his father, Thomas Jefferson Coolidge III, 1986.71.; pp. 28-29 Private Collection/Archives Charmet/Bridgeman Images; p. 35 NARA; pp. 36-37 Musee Franco-Americaine, Blerancourt, Chauny, France/Roger-Viollet, Paris/Bridgeman Images; pp. 39, 40 Courtesy of the Independence National Historical Park Collection, Philadelphia; p. 47 © North Wind Picture Archives; p. 53 Rare Book and Special Collections Division/Library of Congress, Washington, D.C. (http://lccn.loc.gov/02005383); pp. 54-55 Library of Congress, Washington, D.C.; p. 63 National Geographic Creative/Bridgeman Images

CONTENTS

INTRODUCTION

In the mid-1800s there arose in the United States a political and philosophical belief that it was the country's divinely assigned mission to expand westward across North America. In the process, it would spread democratic and Protestant ideals. This belief was called Manifest Destiny.

John O'Sullivan, a journalist, used the phrase in an 1845 editorial about the annexation of Texas, in which he spoke of America's "manifest destiny to overspread the continent allotted by Providence for the free development of our multiplying millions." This was probably the first use of the phrase "manifest destiny," but the roots of the concept can be traced much further back to the colonial period.

One of the grievances that led to the American Revolution was the attempt by Britain to prevent colonists from settling beyond the Appalachian Mountains. As soon as the Revolution had been won, the new government of the United States started making plans for the addition of new states. The American frontier moved in stages. After the Revolution, pioneers gradually crossed the Appalachians and went into the Ohio and Mississippi river valleys. Then, in the mid-1800s, they ventured across the Mississippi River and into the West.

In *American Progress* (*c.* 1873; color print), an allegorical female figure of America leads pioneers and railroads westward, in accordance with the concept of Manifest Destiny.

The most significant event of the expansion period came in 1803, when the United States bought the enormous western territory called Louisiana from France. The Louisiana Purchase doubled the size of the United States and provided a powerful impetus to westward expansion. In 1804 President Thomas Jefferson sent Meriwether Lewis and William Clark on an expedition to explore the Louisiana Purchase and the Pacific Northwest. Lewis and Clark led their party up the Missouri River to its source. Then they crossed the Rocky Mountains—the western boundary of the Louisiana Territory—and went down the Columbia River to the Pacific coast.

Soon American settlers and traders began to travel over the route Lewis and Clark had blazed. Other hardy Americans made their own trails through and beyond the Rockies. The pioneers pushing toward the Southwest and the Pacific coast braved the hostility of foreign powers. Mexico owned both Texas and California and the British had a strong claim to Oregon. In each case the Americans first penetrated and then won complete control of the area. With the admission of California to the Union in 1850, the United States finally stretched from the Atlantic to the Pacific. Its Manifest Destiny had been realized.

The American frontier was an escape and a place of hope for those willing and able to take their futures into their own hands. Celebrated then and ever since in poetry, short stories, novels, drama, films, music, and paintings, the epic westward movement in the United States has never failed to stir the imagination. At the same time, the westward push brought devastation to the original inhabitants of the land—the Native Americans. The bold adventurousness of the pioneers and the brutal clash of cultures make the period of expansion both one of the most exciting and most tragic chapters in American history.

CHAPTER ONE

EUROPEAN EXPLORATION AND SETTLEMENT OF LOUISIANA

The early history of the land that would become Louisiana is dominated by the French. Although the Spanish first explored the region in the 1540s, it was the French who later settled it. They made it part of their North American colony known as New France, which stretched from eastern Canada in the north to the Gulf of Mexico in the south.

Yet for all the vast territory that France laid claim to in North America, New France was never effectively colonized. Many permanent communities were founded, but the main interest of the mother country was commercial exploitation, especially the fur trade. Under French and later Spanish rule, all these settlements, including Baton Rouge and New Orleans in Louisiana, remained frontier outposts. Only after 1800, when citizens of the United States began trekking westward in search of plentiful, inexpensive land, did they really grow.

FRENCH EXPLORATION OF LOUISIANA

During the 17th century a great number of Frenchmen—traders, missionaries, and soldiers—traversed the wilderness from eastern Canada to New Orleans. They ventured throughout the Great Lakes region and the Mississippi River valley, claiming the territory for the king of France. The most famous of these explorers was René-Robert Cavelier, sieur (lord) de La Salle. The father of the Louisiana Territory, La Salle was the first European to voyage down the Mississippi River to the Gulf of Mexico. As a result of this 1682 expedition, France laid claim to the entire Mississippi Valley. La Salle named the territory "Louisiana" for the French king Louis XIV.

France's claim to Louisiana was strengthened by the efforts of

In this print, published in Edward Sylvester Ellis's *The History of Our Country* (1899), Sieur de La Salle lays claim to the entire Mississippi Valley in the name of France.

LA SALLE'S EXPEDITIONS

La Salle's exploration of the Mississippi in 1682 was not his first expedition in North America. Committed to expanding New France, he had sold his land in Montreal to finance an expedition to the Ohio region in 1669–70. A decade later, in 1679, he sailed from Fort Frontenac on Lake Ontario to Green Bay on Lake Michigan. He then continued south, eventually, in 1680, following the Illinois River to its junction with the Mississippi. This was his first glimpse of the river he would famously descend two years later.

After his storied expedition of 1682, La Salle made one more voyage. In 1684 he set out with four ships and about 400 men in an attempt to establish a post at the mouth of the Mississippi. This expedition by sea was doomed from the start. La Salle's naval commander opposed him constantly, and illness took a heavy toll. Many men deserted. Finally, a great miscalculation brought the ships to Matagorda Bay in Texas, 500 miles (800 kilometers) west of their intended landfall. There his naval commander left him with one small ship.

La Salle started to build a fort and made several fruitless journeys in search of his lost Mississippi. His ship was wrecked, and he lost all but 36 of his men. In March 1687 he was murdered by three of his men near the Brazos River in what is now eastern Texas. His vision of a French empire died with him. It would be up to other Frenchmen to colonize New France.

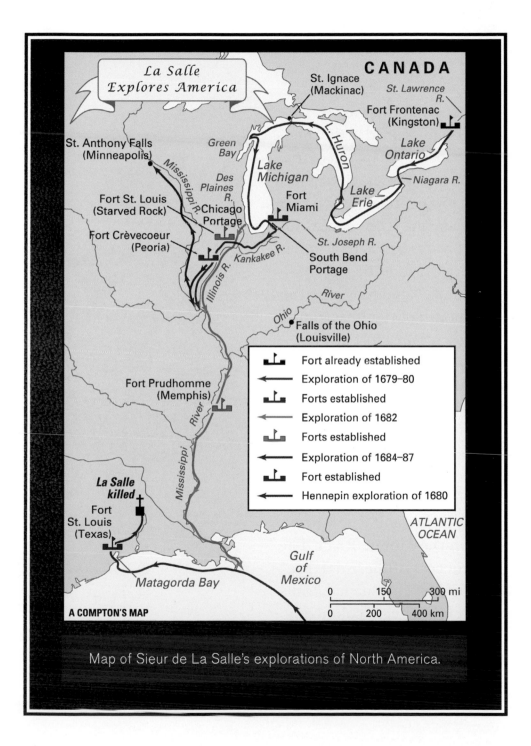

Map of Sieur de La Salle's explorations of North America.

Pierre Le Moyne, sieur d'Iberville. A French-Canadian naval hero and explorer, Iberville was commissioned in the 1690s to locate the mouth of the Mississippi and to establish a fort in order to secure the claim made by La Salle. In 1699 he explored the northern coast of the Gulf of Mexico, rediscovering the mouth of the Mississippi. He set up a fort at what is now Ocean Springs, Mississippi, near Biloxi. This became France's foothold in Louisiana. A year later he established a second fort near the site of present-day New Orleans, and in 1702 he built a new fort on the Mobile River. The success of these defense projects persuaded Louis XIV to begin colonizing Louisiana.

Iberville was accompanied on his Louisiana expedition by his brother Jean-Baptiste Le Moyne, sieur de Bienville. Following

An engraving depicts Sieur de Bienville overseeing work at the site of New Orleans. In 1722 Bienville declared New Orleans the capital of the French colony of Louisiana.

EARLY NEW ORLEANS

Bienville, the French founder of New Orleans, envisioned the settlement becoming a great commercial center. This happened but not without many obstacles. The early settlers battled deadly floods, storms, and yellow fever epidemics plus a constant barrage of insects, snakes, and alligators.

The first residents were a colorful mixture of Canadian backwoodsmen, company craftsmen and troops, convicts, slaves, and political exiles. In a census taken in November 1721, New Orleans had a population of 470 people: 277 whites and 172 black and 21 Indian slaves. The first buildings of the city were crude structures of cypress slabs and mud chink (caulk) topped with thatched roofs. In spite of the primitive homes and muddy surroundings, the wealthier of the residents filled their homes with finery brought from France and dressed accordingly in silk and satin.

The inclination toward a lavish display of wealth was encouraged during French rule of New Orleans. Balls, parties, and banquets became everyday occurrences in the muddy frontier settlement. In addition, a tradition of corruption and graft was established, thus perpetuating the city's already notorious reputation of decadence and immorality.

When the Spanish took possession of the city in 1762, New Orleans was floundering economically. After a brief rebellion by the Creoles, as the French settlers were known, the residents of New Orleans enjoyed peace and a growing prosperity under Spanish rule.

Iberville's death in 1706, Bienville carried on his efforts to develop the Louisiana colony. He served multiple terms as colonial governor, contending with disease, hostile Native Americans, and enemies among his own countrymen. His vigorous leadership enabled the colony to survive. In 1718 he founded New Orleans, and four years later he made that city the new capital of the colony.

FRENCH AND INDIAN WAR

In the late 1600s into the 1700s France and England were engaged in a struggle for North America. They vied for control of land, the fur trade, and the American Indians. There was also bitter hostility between France and England in Europe. Between 1689 and 1748 the two powers waged three separate wars—King William's War, Queen Anne's War, and King George's War—for supremacy in North America. In each of these conflicts, both the French and the British were helped by their Indian allies.

At first, most of the fighting in North America between England and France was centered in the New England–New York areas. Later a new front, the upper Ohio River valley, was opened. Here the important French and Indian War began in 1754. It pitted the English, allied with the Iroquois, against a much larger coalition made up of many Algonquian-speaking tribes, the French, and the Spanish. Two years later

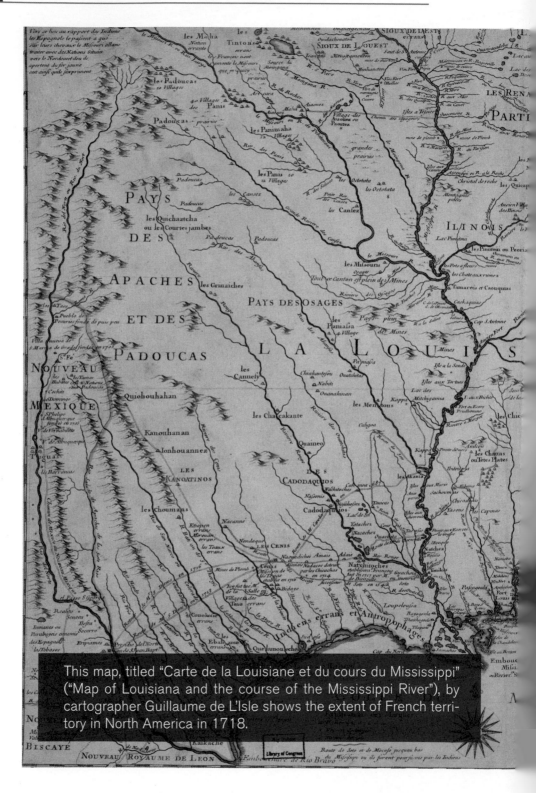

This map, titled "Carte de la Louisiane et du cours du Mississippi" ("Map of Louisiana and the course of the Mississippi River"), by cartographer Guillaume de L'Isle shows the extent of French territory in North America in 1718.

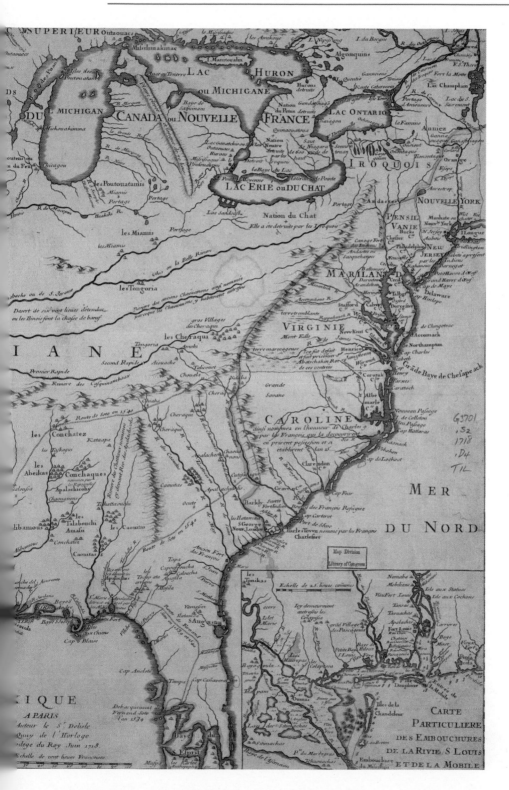

Although ultimately victorious in the French and Indian War, the British struggled until 1758, when the tides of war turned in their favor. Illustrated here is General Edward Braddock being carried away after an ambush by the French and their Indian allies in 1755. Braddock would later die from his wounds.

the conflict spread to Europe, where it was known as the Seven Years' War.

The war came about when the French began building a chain of forts from the St. Lawrence River to the Mississippi. This land was claimed by Virginia under its 1609 colonial charter from England. In 1754 Virginia sent a small force under young George Washington to capture Fort Duquesne, a French post located on the present site of Pittsburgh, Pennsylvania, but he was defeated.

The next year, 1755, was still more disastrous for the British. Advancing on Fort Duquesne, General Edward Braddock and his army were ambushed by the French and their Indian allies. Braddock was killed, and only Washington's skillful tactics saved the army from being wiped out.

The French continued to dominate the war until 1758, when the tide turned. That year the British prime minister, William Pitt the Elder, sent out a well-equipped army and fleet assisted by colonial troops. They captured several key French forts. In 1759, in one of the great battles of the war, the British captured the French stronghold of Quebec. In 1760 Montreal surrendered. This ended French resistance in Canada, and France faced certain defeat. It then secretly ceded to Spain the city of New Orleans and all land west of the Mississippi River—the Louisiana Territory.

LOUISIANA UNDER SPAIN

The transfer of Louisiana to Spain established nearly four decades of Spanish rule and influence in the area. In 1779 the Spanish wrested Baton Rouge from the British and took all of West Florida, which then extended from the peninsula westward across the Gulf Coast to the Mississippi River. After the American Revolution hardy Western boatmen and traders began shipping produce into New Orleans. High customs duties and Spanish threats to close the port angered the Americans.

French power rebounded under the military leadership of Napoleon Bonaparte. On October 1, 1800,
Napoleon persuaded a hesitant King Charles IV of

The Cabildo in New Orleans was the seat of colonial government during the period of
Spanish rule of the Louisiana Territory. Built between 1795 and 1799, it hosted the
formal transfer of the Louisiana Purchase from France to the United States in 1803.

Spain to cede Louisiana back to France. King Charles verbally agreed, on the condition that France would never turn the territory over to a third power—a condition that did not carry over into the written treaty.

At the time of Louisiana's return to France, most of the people in the territory lived along the Red and Mississippi rivers. New Orleans was the chief settlement, with a population of about 10,000. In just a few years this coveted port—along with the rest of Louisiana—would change hands once again.

CHAPTER TWO

THE LOUISIANA PURCHASE

The United States did not differ from European countries in wanting to expand its control to its "natural boundaries." American settlers west of the Appalachians wanted New Orleans very much. The country that controlled New Orleans could control the Mississippi River. Western farmers were eager for this control to be in the hands of the United States. Their grain, hogs, cattle, and other produce were sent to market by flatboats that floated down the great "Father of Waters."

Because of the strategic importance of the river and the port, the U.S. government was deeply concerned about the return of Louisiana to the French in 1800. In 1795 Spain and the United States had signed a treaty that gave the United States the right to ship goods originating in American ports through the mouth of the Mississippi without paying duty. The treaty also granted the United States the right of deposit, or temporary storage, of American goods at New Orleans. The transfer of Louisiana from Spain to France was bad news for the western farmers. France was then the most powerful country in the world, and there was no hope of forcing any privileges from it.

JEFFERSON BUYS LOUISIANA

Napoleon's dream of a vast colonial empire vanished, however, almost as suddenly as it had come. At the time France was embroiled in a series of wars against shifting alliances of other European powers. Napoleon, determined to enhance French influence and territory, led the French military to great victories on the battlefield in the late 1790s. In 1798, however, he suffered a major failure when Britain defeated the French navy in the Battle of the Nile. Meanwhile France was fighting a losing battle against a rebellion of the black population in its Caribbean colony of Saint-Domingue (Haiti).

France's troubles proved to be an opportunity for the United States. U.S. President Thomas Jefferson instructed Robert R. Livingston, the U.S. minister in Paris, to take two steps: (1) to approach Napoleon's minister, Charles Maurice de Talleyrand, to try to prevent the return of Louisiana to France in the event it had not yet been completed; and (2) to try to purchase at least New Orleans if the property had actually been transferred from Spain to France. Direct negotiations with Talleyrand, however, appeared to be all but impossible. For months Livingston had to be content with slim hopes of a possible deal between France and the United States.

Even these hopes faded when Livingston learned that Spain withdrew the right of deposit at New

Thomas Jefferson.

Orleans in 1802. He had good reasons for thinking the worst—that Napoleon may have been responsible for the unfortunate act and that his next move might be to close the Mississippi River entirely to the Americans. Aware of France's hostility toward the British, Livingston used this to his advantage in his negotiations with the French. He made it known that reconciliation with Britain might, after all, best serve the interests of the United States, and at that moment a U.S.-British alliance was the least of Napoleon's desires.

There are good reasons to believe that French failure to hold onto Saint-Domingue, the possibility of renewed war with Britain, and financial difficulties may all have prompted Napoleon to negotiate a deal with the United States. At this point, James Monroe arrived in France with power from President Jefferson to assist Livingston in

Illustrated here is the burning of the city of Cap-Francais in the French colony of Saint-Dominique. The revolution in France's most important Caribbean colony may have been one reason Napoleon was willing to sell Louisiana to the United States.

the purchase of only New Orleans and East and West Florida for not more than $10 million. However, Monroe and Livingston were offered the whole of the French territory for approximately $15 million. Although the American agents had no authority to spend such a large sum, they signed the treaty of purchase on May 2, 1803 (though it was backdated to April 30, 1803). The area involved was a vast 828,000 square miles (2,145,000 square kilometers). Thus at one stroke the size of the United States was doubled.

The price of the Louisiana Purchase was only a tiny fraction of its value today. At less than three cents per acre, it was the greatest land bargain in U.S. history.

OXFORD·PRINT·BOSTON

MESSRS. MON

THE LOUISIANA PURCHASE.
LIVINGSTONE COMPLETING NEGOTIATIONS WITH TALLYRAND, APRIL 30, 1803

COPYRIGHT 1904, C. H. NICHOLS.

James Monroe and Robert R. Livingston, representing the United States, negotiate the Louisiana Purchase with Charles Maurice de Talleyrand of France.

DEFINING THE PURCHASE

Precisely what the United States had purchased was unclear. The wording of the treaty was vague. It did not clearly describe boundaries. It did not give any guarantee that West Florida was to be considered a part of Louisiana, nor did it specify the southwest boundary. The American negotiators were fully aware of this.

The setting of fixed boundaries awaited negotiations with Spain and Britain. The dispute with Spain over the ownership of West Florida and Texas was settled by the purchase of the Floridas from Spain in 1819 and the establishment of a boundary line dividing the

British Territory

Spanish Territory

PACIFIC OCEAN

W

0   2

0   200

Great Lakes

New Hampshire
Vermont
Maine

Massachusetts

New York

Rhode Island
Connecticut
New Jersey

Penn.

Delaware

LOUISIANA PURCHASE

Indiana Territory

Ohio

Virginia

Maryland

Kentucky

North Carolina

Tennessee

South Carolina

Mississippi Territory

Georgia

ATLANTIC OCEAN

Spanish Florida

E

400 miles

kilometers

Gulf of Mexico

© 2006 Encyclopædia Britannica, Inc.

Map of the territory of the United States at the time of the Louisiana Purchase. The purchase doubled the size of the United States, adding approximately 828,000 square miles (2,145,000 square kilometers) of land to the relatively young nation.

CONSTITUTIONALITY OF THE LOUISIANA PURCHASE

Before the United States could establish fixed boundaries for Louisiana, a basic question arose concerning whether or not the Louisiana Purchase had been constitutional. Did the U.S. Constitution provide for an act of this kind? President Jefferson–a strict constructionist–believed that the annexation and government of such a vast territory was unconstitutional. He wanted an amendment to the Constitution to ratify it. The members of his Cabinet did not think an amendment was necessary, and their views prevailed. The New England Federalists were enraged at the prospect of the admission of numerous new states whose votes in the Senate and House of Representatives would reinforce those of the South and West. However, after due consideration and considerable discussion, the Senate approved the treaty by a vote of 24 to 7.

two countries' claims. This line ran from the southeastern corner of what is now Louisiana, north and west to what is now Wyoming, and then west along the latitude 42° N to the Pacific Ocean. The northern boundary was established by an agreement with the British in 1818. It established the 49° parallel N

In December 1803 the American flag was raised over New Orleans for the first time in a ceremony marking the transfer of the Louisiana Territory to the United States.

between the Lake of the Woods and the Rocky Mountains as the American-Canadian border. The Rockies were accepted as the western limit of the Louisiana Territory, and the Mississippi River was considered for all practical purposes the eastern boundary of the great purchase.

Much of the territory acquired in the Louisiana Purchase turned out to contain rich mineral resources, good soil, valuable grazing land, forests, and wild-life resources of great value. Out of this territory were carved the entire states of Missouri, Arkansas, Iowa, North Dakota, South Dakota, Nebraska, and Oklahoma, as well as Louisiana. In addition, the Louisiana Purchase included most of the land in what are now the states of Kansas, Colorado, Wyoming, Montana, and Minnesota.

CHAPTER THREE

LEWIS AND CLARK EXPEDITION

A t the start of the 1800s American settlers knew little about western North America. In 1792 Captain Robert Gray, an American navigator, had sailed up the mouth of the great river he named the Columbia. Traders and trappers reported that the source of the Missouri River was in the mountains in the Far West. No one, however, had yet blazed an overland trail.

President Jefferson was interested in knowing more about the country west of the Mississippi and in finding a water route to the Pacific Ocean. He also wanted to make diplomatic contact with Native American groups in the area and to expand the U.S. fur trade. In 1803 he asked Congress for $2,500 for an expedition.

THE EXPLORERS

To head the expedition, Jefferson chose his young secretary, Captain Meriwether Lewis. Lewis invited

his friend Lieutenant William Clark to share the
leadership. Both were familiar with the frontier and
with some Native American groups through their
service in the army.

William Clark, portrait by Charles Willson Peale, *c.* 1807; in
Independence National Historical Park, Philadelphia.

Before Lewis and Clark set out, word came of the Louisiana Purchase. Therefore, part of the region the expedition would be exploring was U.S. territory.

Meriwether Lewis, portrait by Charles Willson Peale, c. 1807–08; in Independence National Historical Park, Philadelphia.

Plans for the expedition were carefully laid. The party was to ascend the Missouri River to its source, carry canoes across the Continental Divide, and descend the Columbia River to its mouth. In preparation for the historic journey, Lewis studied natural history and learned how to fix latitude and longitude by the stars. In the winter of 1803–04 the expedition was assembled in Illinois, near St. Louis. The permanent party originally consisted of the two leaders, Lewis and Clark; three sergeants; 22 privates; the part–Native American frontiersman George Drouillard;

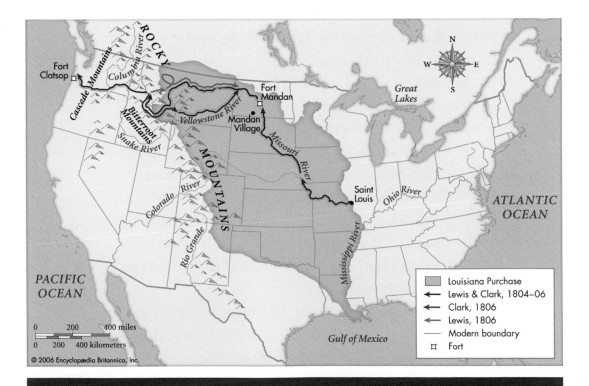

Map showing the Louisiana Purchase and the routes of the Lewis and Clark Expedition of 1804–06.

and Clark's African American slave, York. They called themselves the Corps of Discovery.

TO THE PACIFIC

On May 14, 1804, the explorers started up the Missouri in a 55-foot (17-meter) covered keelboat and two small canoes, paddled by French boatmen and a small temporary escort. On August 3 they held their first meeting with Native Americans—the Oto and Missouri—at a place the explorers named Council Bluff, across the river and downstream from present-day Council Bluffs, Iowa. In late October they reached the earth-lodge villages of the Mandan, near the present site of Bismarck, North Dakota.

Across the river from the Mandan villages, the explorers built Fort Mandan and spent the winter. It was there that they hired Toussaint Charbonneau, a French Canadian interpreter, and his Shoshone wife, Sacagawea, the sister of a Shoshone chief. While at Fort Mandan, Sacagawea gave birth to a baby boy. This did not stop her from participating in the group. She carried the child on her back for the rest of the trip. As a Shoshone interpreter she proved invaluable.

In the spring of 1805 the keelboat was sent back to St. Louis with dispatches for President Jefferson and with natural history specimens. Meanwhile, canoes had been built. On April 7 the party—which now included 33 people—continued up the Missouri. On April 26 it passed the mouth of the Yellowstone River, and on June 13 it reached the Great Falls of the Missouri. Carrying the laden canoes 18 miles (29 kilometers) around the falls caused a month's delay. In mid-July the canoes were launched again above the falls. Later that month the expedition reached Three Forks, where three rivers join to form the Missouri. They named the rivers the Madison, the Jefferson, and the Gallatin, after presidents James Madison and Thomas Jefferson, and Albert Gallatin, who was secretary of treasury under Jefferson.

For some time the explorers had been within sight of the Rocky Mountains. Crossing them was to be the hardest part of the journey. The expedition decided to follow the Jefferson River, the fork that led westward toward the mountains.

On August 12 Lewis climbed to the top of the Continental Divide, where he hoped to see the headwaters of the Columbia close enough to let them carry their canoes and proceed downstream toward the Pacific. Instead he saw mountains stretching endlessly into the distance. The water route that Jefferson had sent them to find did not exist.

They were now in the country of the Shoshone. Sacagawea eagerly watched for her people, but it was Lewis who found them. The chief, Sacagawea's brother, provided the party with horses and a guide for the difficult crossing of the lofty Bitterroot Range.

THE LIFE OF SACAGAWEA

Sacagawea, a Native American of the Shoshone tribe, served as an interpreter for the Lewis and Clark Expedition when she was just a teenager. She traveled thousands of miles through the wilderness with the explorers, from the Dakotas to the Pacific Ocean and back again. Many memorials have been raised in her honor, in part for the fortitude with which she faced hardship on the difficult journey.

Separating fact from legend in Sacagawea's life is difficult. Historians disagree on the dates of her birth and death and even on her name. One version of her name, Sacagawea, means "Bird Woman" in the Hidatsa language. Alternatively, her name is sometimes spelled Sacajawea or Sakakawea. She is thought to have been born in about 1788, near the Continental Divide at what is now the Idaho-Montana border. In about 1800, when she was about 12 years old, a raiding party of the Hidatsa people captured her near the headwaters of the Missouri River. The Hidatsa made her a slave and took her to the Mandan-Hidatsa villages near what is now Bismarck, North Dakota. In about 1804 she became one of the wives of the French Canadian fur trader Toussaint Charbonneau. (Sacagawea may have been sold to him.)

Sacagawea was not the guide for the Lewis and Clark Expedition, as some have wrongly portrayed her. She did, however, recognize landmarks in southwestern Montana. She also informed Clark that Bozeman

Pass was the best route between the Missouri and Yellowstone rivers on their return journey. Sacagawea and her family left the expedition when they arrived back at the Mandan-Hidatsa villages.

It is believed that Sacagawea died shortly after giving birth to a daughter on December 20, 1812, at Fort Manuel, near what is now Mobridge, South Dakota. Clark became the legal guardian of her two children.

In the years since her death, Sacagawea has become a legend, the subject of many books and movies. She has also been honored with monuments, statues, U.S. postage stamps, and a U.S. dollar coin. In 2001 she was given the title of honorary sergeant in the regular U.S. army.

It took the Corps of Discovery most of September to cross the mountains. Hungry, sick, and exhausted, they reached a point on the Clearwater River where Nez Percé Indians helped them make dugout canoes. From there they were able to proceed by water. They reached the Columbia River on October 16.

On November 7, 1805, after a journey of nearly 18 months, Clark wrote in his journal, "Great joy in camp. We are now in view of the Ocean." They reached the Pacific later that month. They were disappointed to find no ships at the mouth of the Columbia. A few miles from the Pacific shore, south of present-day Astoria, Oregon, they built a stockade, Fort Clatsop. There they spent the rainy winter.

The Lewis and Clark Expedition travels on the Columbia River.

RETURN

On March 23, 1806, the entire party started back. They crossed the mountains in June with Nez Percé horses and guides. Beside the Bitterroot River the two leaders separated to learn more about the country. Clark headed for the Yellowstone River and followed it to the

Missouri. Lewis, with nine men, struck off toward the northeast to explore a branch of the Missouri that he named the Marias. On this trip he had a skirmish with Native Americans that left two Blackfeet dead, the only such incident of the entire journey. Later, while out hunting, he was accidentally shot by one of his own men. He recovered after the party was reunited and had stopped at the Mandan villages. There they left Sacagawea and her family.

The party reached St. Louis on September 23, 1806. Their arrival caused great rejoicing, for they had been

Much of what is known about the Lewis and Clark Expedition comes from the extensive journals kept by the explorers. Shown here is a spread of the handwritten notes of William Clark.

ZEBULON PIKE

Although certainly the most commemorated, Lewis and Clark were not the only explorers sent out into the vast territory acquired in the Louisiana Purchase. In the winter of 1805 another explorer named Zebulon Pike was sent up the Mississippi River from St. Louis to find the river's source. He did not discover the real source. It is in a district of lakes and swamps that was then under thick ice and snow. He did, however, bring back much information about the country above the mouth of the St. Peter's, or Minnesota, River.

In the summer of 1806 Pike was sent out again, this time to find the sources of the Red River and the Arkansas River. Again he found neither, but he saw the great peak that has come to be known as Pikes Peak. He also visited the place where the Rio Grande rises in southern Colorado. Here he was arrested by Spanish soldiers for trespassing on Spanish territory. In 1807 he was returned unharmed to the American army post at Natchitoches, in what is now Louisiana. He published a book a little later that aroused the ambition of traders on the Missouri border to visit Santa Fe and capture the markets of the Spanish settlers.

General Pike?

Zebulon Pike.

believed dead. They had been gone two years, four months, and nine days and had traveled nearly 8,000 miles (13,000 kilometers).

Lewis, Clark, and several other members of the expedition kept detailed journals. They brought back much new material for cartographers and specimens of previously unknown wildlife. American settlers and traders soon began to travel over the route they had blazed. The expedition also provided useful support for the U.S. claim to the Oregon country.

LEGACY OF THE LEWIS AND CLARK EXPEDITION

Some insist Lewis and Clark's legacy is insignificant because they were not the first non-Indians to explore the area, they did not find an all-water route across the continent, and they failed to publish their journals in a timely fashion. Although the first official account appeared in 1814, the two-volume narrative did not contain any of their scientific achievements. Nevertheless, the expedition contributed significant geographic and scientific knowledge of the West, aided the expansion of the fur trade, and strengthened U.S. claims to the Pacific. Clark's maps portraying the geography of the West, printed in 1810 and 1814, were the best available until the 1840s.

No American exploration looms larger in U.S. history. The Lewis and Clark Expedition has been commemorated with stamps, monuments, and trails and has had numerous places named after it. St. Louis hosted the 1904 World's Fair during the expedition's centennial, and Portland, Oregon, sponsored the 1905 Lewis and Clark Exposition. In 1978 Congress established the 3,700-mile (6,000-kilometer) Lewis and Clark National Historic Trail. While Lewis and Clark had a

The Sacagawea dollar coin was released in 2000 to commemorate the Shoshone interpreter who provided invaluable help to Lewis and Clark on their expedition.

great interest in documenting Native American cultures, they represented a government whose policies can now be seen to have fostered dispossession and cultural genocide. This dichotomy was on display during the event's bicentennial, commemorated by two years of special events across the expedition route.

CHAPTER FOUR

WESTWARD EXPANSION AND ITS EFFECTS

A fter the Lewis and Clark Expedition, the general area of the Far West was known. However, there was no rush of settlers to occupy it. Louisiana became a state in 1812, and Missouri did so in 1821. Three more states along the Mississippi— Arkansas (1836), Iowa (1846), and Minnesota (1858)— were admitted in time. West of Missouri there was no serious move for a new state until after 1850.

Meanwhile the United States accepted the verdict of early explorers. Their opinion was that farmers could not make settlements in the country west of the states along the Mississippi. Resources were deemed scarce and the land unforgiving. Schoolbooks called it the Great American Desert. The farming frontier developed east of the Mississippi and in the new states west of it. For

An illustration by Karl Bodmer shows Plains Indians hunting bison in the 1830s.

several decades more the Far West remained mainly a land of Native Americans and wild game.

MISSIONARIES AND TRADERS

Long before Americans explored the Far West, the country had been known to the French and Spanish. Missionary explorers and soldiers had visited it many

times. From New Orleans traders had worked their way up the
river to St. Louis. From St. Louis
they had reached out toward the
Rocky Mountains, persuading
Native Americans to bring in
furs and sending out trappers
to collect them. The traders'
runners knew many details of
the Great Plains long before
surveyors arrived to map it.

When the Far West became
part of the United States, the
government wanted to protect
the fur trade for American citizens. It tried to drive out foreign
trappers. Stockaded posts were
built for agency houses, where
trade with the Native Americans
was carried on. Around many
of the posts, the cabins of these
trappers and their families
were the beginnings of white
occupation.

From 1812 to 1846 the fur
trade was the chief resource of
the Far West. The great region
seemed destined to continue a
wild land.

PARSONS. DEL.

Fort Astoria (now Astoria, Oregon) was a fur-trading post founded by John Jacob Astor near the mouth of the Columbia River. The illustration shows the fort in 1813.

THE OREGON COUNTRY

To the northwest lay the Oregon country, valued for its furs and as a way station for ships in the China trade. Oregon was subject to the claims of both Britain and the United States. It was held in joint occupation until the owners could agree how to divide it. The United States became interested in the early 1830s, when trappers began to send parties up the Missouri and the Platte rivers and into the valleys of the Columbia. Missionary societies began sending missions to the Native Americans.

In the spring of 1843 there gathered near the bend of the Missouri River, on the eastern edge of the Indian country, more than 1,000 homeseekers. They were determined to risk the long and dangerous overland trip for the sake of farmland in Oregon. In 1846 Britain and the United States divided the Oregon country along the line of 49° N latitude. The overland trails took on new importance. To the Native Americans the trails were a calamity. They carried thousands of whites into the territory. To the farmers of the Midwest, they were the channel to the greatest long-distance migration in American history.

THE OREGON TRAIL

The chief and most famous of the routes to the West was the Oregon Trail. It began at the stretch of the Missouri River where the stream turns sharply eastward at the mouth of the Kansas River. Each spring overland emigrants gathered along the Missouri above the bend. They completed their outfits at the stores near Independence, Missouri. When the prairie began to show green, they rushed to head their wagon trains northwestward.

The main highway, well trodden by 1846, began at Independence and Westport Landing (now Kansas City). It ran cross-country to Fort Kearney, on the Platte River. The fort was built to protect the travelers and to outfit them. The main Oregon Trail followed the south bank of the Platte to the junction of the North and South forks. It then followed the south bank of the North Platte through Mitchell Pass to Fort Laramie, at the mouth of the Laramie River. A band of religious emigrants, the Mormons, ascended the Platte in 1847. They followed the north bank, thereafter known as the Mormon Trail.

Both trails merged as one along the Sweetwater branch of the North Platte. Beyond the head of the Sweetwater the wagons crossed the Continental Divide through South Pass. West of South Pass the Oregon Trail followed the Snake River, passing Fort Hall and Fort Boise in what is now Idaho. From Fort Walla Walla the Trail followed the south bank of the Columbia to an area near Fort Vancouver. Most of the travelers left the Trail there and settled in the Willamette Valley. Some, however, followed the Columbia on to the Pacific coast.

The Trail was bordered with the graves of those who died along the way as well as discarded goods, abandoned

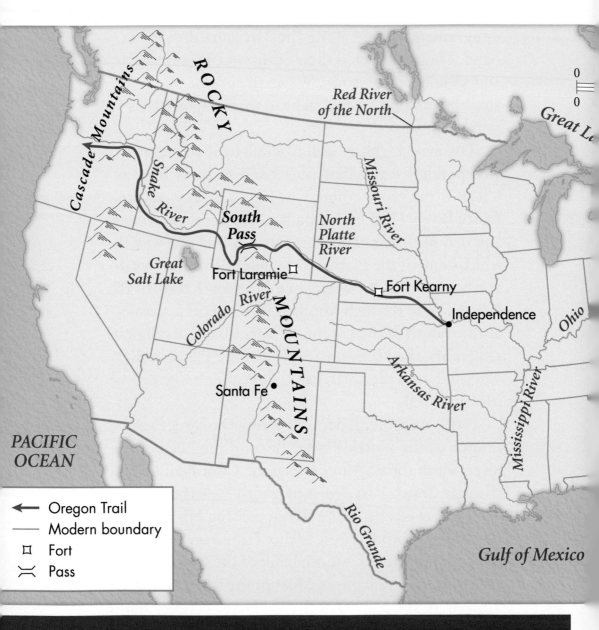

ROCKY

Cascade Mountains

Snake River

South Pass

Great Salt Lake

Fort Laramie

Colorado River

Santa Fe

MOUNTAINS

Red River of the North

Missouri River

North Platte River

Fort Kearny

Independence

Arkansas River

Rio Grande

Great L

Ohio

Mississippi River

PACIFIC OCEAN

Gulf of Mexico

0
0

← Oregon Trail
— Modern boundary
⌗ Fort
)⚬(Pass

The Oregon Trail began in the U.S. state of Missouri and ended in what is now Oregon.

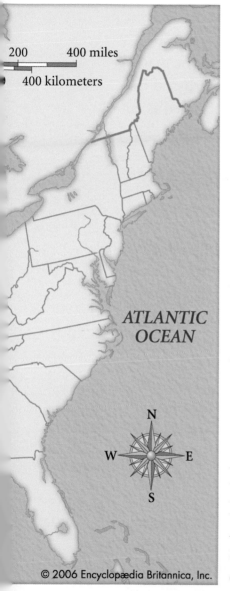

broken wagons, and skeletons of horses and oxen. Thousands of people followed the Oregon Trail into Oregon. In 1848 Congress created the Oregon Territory, parts of which eventually became the states of Oregon and Washington.

At the same time, many homeseekers were moving toward California. These settlers followed the Oregon Trail as far as Soda Springs (in what is now Idaho). There they turned southwestward toward California.

THE SANTA FE TRAIL

Southwest from the bend of the Missouri, the Santa Fe Trail crossed the Great Plains to New Mexico. Regular use of the Trail began after Mexico gained independence from Spain in 1821. Wagons began to cross the Kansas plains to the great bend of the Arkansas River. The main route ascended the river to the mouth of the Purgatoire, near La Junta in Colorado. It then continued to the town of Santa Fe.

The Santa Fe Trail—and its extension to California, the Spanish Trail—was not an emigrant road. It was used chiefly by traders. Their wagons full of goods raced across the Plains and followed the market down the Rio Grande. Sometimes they crossed the Chihuahua Desert below El Paso and penetrated as far south as Mexico City.

THE "INDIAN PROBLEM" AND U.S. POLICY

During the westward expansion, settlers and the U.S. government treated the American Indians as an obstacle to be overcome. The government's method of dealing with the "Indian problem" evolved over the years. Beginning in the 1770s, the government negotiated treaties with a number of Indian tribes. Typically the tribes agreed to turn over much of their land to the United States in exchange for money, goods, and promises that U.S. citizens would not settle in the tribes' remaining territory. These treaties were considered to be agreements between two sovereign nations. Nevertheless, the terms were routinely violated as settlers continued to trespass on Indian lands. The result was decades of conflict between Indians and the U.S. government.

The most dramatic of the Indians' struggles to hold their lands against white settlers was the one led by the Shawnee leader Tecumseh. As settlers flooded into Indian territory following the Louisiana Purchase,

Tecumseh organized a confederation of tribes to resist further settlement. In 1811 a group of Shawnee led by Tecumseh's brother Tenskwatawa were defeated by General William Henry Harrison, the future U.S. president, at the Battle of Tippecanoe in Indiana.

After the War of 1812, with the United States secure in its borders, the federal government no longer treated the Indians as peoples of separate nations. Rather, they were considered wards of the United States, to be relocated at the convenience of the government. In 1830 this policy was made law when President Andrew Jackson signed the Indian Removal Act. The act authorized the president to remove tribes from their land east of the Mississippi and resettle them west of the river. The federal government aggressively followed a policy of resettlement in the Indian Territory (later the state of Oklahoma). The eastern Indian tribes were driven westward along the Trail of Tears.

THE MEXICAN-AMERICAN WAR AND THE SLAVERY QUESTION

In 1845 the United States admitted Texas as a state. The annexation led to trouble, as the United States and Mexico disagreed over the boundary separating the two countries. This brought a declaration of war on May 13, 1846. In less than a year and a half American forces conquered California, the New Mexico region, and northern Mexico. The Treaty of Guadalupe-Hidalgo

THE TRAIL OF TEARS

During the 1830s the U.S. government forced some 100,000 American Indians to leave their homes in the East and move to new lands west of the Mississippi River. Most of the Indians had to make the grueling journey on foot. About 15,000 died during the trip, which is remembered as the Trail of Tears. The term is used most commonly to describe the experience of the Southeast Indians in general and the Cherokee people in particular.

Following the passage of the Indian Removal Act of 1830, the Cherokee resisted removal by turning to the U.S. courts. Their lawsuits reached the U.S. Supreme Court but ultimately were unsuccessful in preventing the tribe's removal. In 1838 the U.S. military began to force Cherokee people from their homes, often at gunpoint. Held in miserable prison camps for days or weeks before their journeys began, many Cherokee became ill, and most were poorly prepared for the very difficult trip. With inadequate food, shelter, and clothing, the Cherokee suffered terribly on the march, especially after cold weather arrived. About 4,000 of the estimated 15,000 Cherokee died on the 116-day journey, many because the escorting troops refused to slow or stop so that the ill and exhausted could recover. In 1987 the U.S. Congress named the Trail of Tears a National Historic Trail in memory of those who suffered and died during removal.

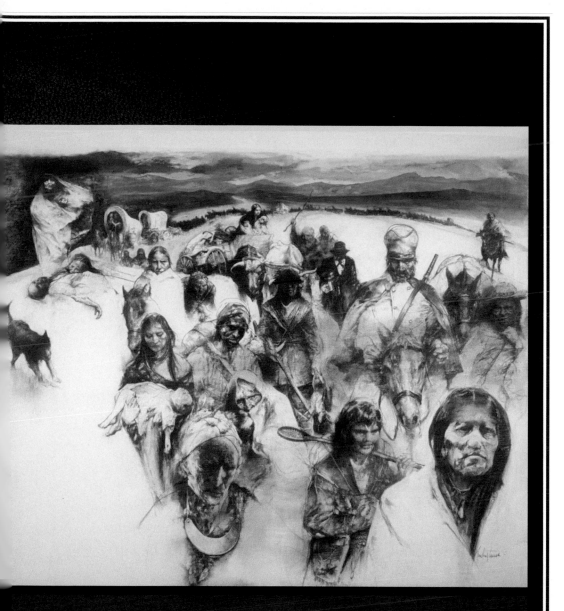

The Cherokee travel the Trail of Tears. Thousands of Native Americans died during the treacherous journey west.

ended the Mexican-American War in 1848. Mexico accepted the Rio Grande river as the international border. It ceded to the United States nearly all the territory that now makes up California, New Mexico, Utah, Nevada, Arizona, Texas, and western Colorado.

The acquisition of the new territories revived the national debate over slavery. Since colonial times, the agricultural economy of the South had been dependent on the labor of black slaves. Although Northern businessmen made great fortunes from the slave trade and from investments in Southern plantations, slavery was never widespread in the North. In the 1800s the cotton industry and the introduction of new machinery brought about an agricultural rebirth in the South, and slavery became more profitable than ever. At the same time, a wave of democratic reform fueled opposition to slavery in the North.

More and more Northerners became convinced that slavery should not be allowed to spread to new territories. At the same time Southerners were becoming equally determined to create new slave states. For 40 years this issue created an ever-widening breach between the South and the rest of the country. The slave states had long been a separate section economically. Now they began to regard themselves as a separate social and political unit as well.

The land acquisition resulting from the Mexican-American War seemed to open new opportunities for the spread of slavery. The Wilmot Proviso, proposed to

Congress in 1846, would have banned slavery from any territories acquired by the United States from Mexico. Although the proposal was not passed, it contributed greatly to rising tensions over the future of slavery in the United States. By 1848 six more states had been admitted to the Union. Three were slave states—Arkansas (1836), Florida (1845), and Texas (1845)—and three were free—Michigan (1837), Iowa (1846), and Wisconsin (1848). This preserved the even balance between the North and South. Each had 15 states.

This balance was threatened, however, by the rapid development of California. In 1848 James Wilson Marshall discovered gold near Coloma. The following

The discovery of gold in California in 1848 and the subsequent gold rush that brought record-high numbers of migrants to the region led to the admission of California as a state—again sparking the debate on the balance of slave states and free states.

year tens of thousands of newcomers made up the historic gold rush of 1849, which broke all records for migration. By the end of the year a state constitution had been adopted. California began asking for admission into the Union as a free state. Throughout the South protest meetings were held. The Northern states were equally insistent that slavery should not be extended.

Just when the slavery issue threatened to break up the Union, Congress passed the Compromise of 1850. It provided that California be admitted as a free state and that New Mexico and Utah be organized as territories without mention of slavery. The Compromise abolished slavery in the District of Columbia but gave the South a stronger fugitive slave law.

BUILDUP TO WAR

The Compromise of 1850 eased the fears of the South only temporarily. The conflict over slavery was renewed when Congress passed the Kansas-Nebraska Act in 1854. This act repealed the Missouri Compromise of 1820, which had prohibited slavery north of latitude 36° 30'. It allowed the people of Kansas and Nebraska to decide for themselves if their territories would allow slavery. The act led to the first armed conflict between North and South. The tension between the two regions was later heightened by the Dred Scott Decision, which held that Congress could not prohibit slavery in federal territories.

By the end of the 1850s, the North feared complete control of the nation by slaveholding interests, and the white South believed that the North was determined to destroy its way of life. White Southerners had been embittered by Northern defiance of the federal Fugitive Slave Act of 1850 and had been alarmed in 1859 by the raid at Harpers Ferry, West Virginia, led by the white abolitionist John Brown. After Abraham Lincoln was elected president in 1860 on the antislavery platform of the new Republican Party, the Southern states seceded from the Union and formed the Confederacy. Civil war was near.

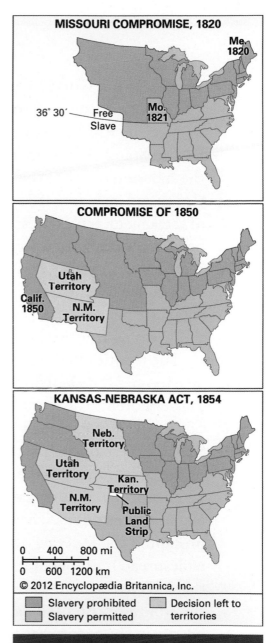

Maps show the compromises over the extension of slavery into the territories after the Missouri Compromise, the Compromise of 1850, and the Kansas-Nebraska Act.

CONCLUSION

In 1893, at the World's Columbian Exhibition in Chicago, historian Frederick Jackson Turner reflected on how the frontier experience had shaped the United States. In his introduction, he noted that the superintendent of the census had stated in 1890: "Up to and including 1880 the country had a frontier of settlement, but at present the unsettled area has been so broken into by isolated bodies of settlement that there can hardly be said to be a frontier line." This quiet statement was in fact an epoch-making announcement. For the first time in American history, there was no frontier.

The frontier had served several purposes in the development of the United States. For one thing, Turner noted, "the frontier promoted the formation of a composite nationality for the American people." Second, the frontier promoted the interdependence of the states. It created a diversified agriculture and made demands on the older communities for manufactured goods. The opening of the West also prompted the federal government to begin the widespread building of roads, canals, and railroads that linked disparate sections of the country. Third, the frontier promoted nationalism in another way. People in the territories did not regard themselves as citizens of a particular state, but as citizens of the United States. Finally, Turner insisted, "the most important effect of the frontier has been the promotion of democracy here and in Europe. . . the frontier individualism has from the beginning promoted democracy."

Thus, decades of American expansionism started by the Louisiana Purchase saw the United States reach its natural western boundary—the Pacific Ocean. While the experience did much to shape a shared American identity, at the same time it exposed divisions that would lead the country to its most dire crisis yet—the Civil War.

TIMELINE

1682 Sieur de la Salle leads a French expedition down the Mississippi River from the Illinois Territory to the Gulf of Mexico, claiming the Mississippi Valley for France.

1699 Sieur d'Iberville sets up a colony near present-day Ocean Springs, Mississippi, which becomes France's foothold in Louisiana.

1718 Sieur de Bienville founds New Orleans, which would become the capital of the Louisiana colony.

1754–1763 British and French forces battle for supremacy in North America in the French and Indian War.

1762 France cedes Louisiana to Spain.

1795 Spain and the United States sign the Treaty of San Lorenzo (also known as Pinckney's Treaty), granting Americans generous trading and shipping rights along the Mississippi.

1800 Spain secretly transfers Louisiana back to France in the Treaty of San Ildefonso.

May 2, 1803 American diplomats Robert R. Livingston and James Monroe sign a treaty to purchase the Louisiana Territory from France.

December 20, 1803 France formally cedes the Louisiana Territory to the United States.

May 1804 The Lewis and Clark Expedition sets out to explore the Louisiana Purchase and the Pacific Northwest.

November 1805 Lewis and Clark reach the Pacific coast near present-day Astoria, Oregon.

September 1806 Lewis and Clark return to St. Louis.

1818–1819 The United States and Britain negotiate the northern boundary of the Louisiana Territory. Spain sells the Floridas to the United States, defining the southwest boundary of the Louisiana Territory.

1830 Congress passes the Indian Removal Act, which requires all Native Americans living east of the Mississippi River to relocate to the West.

1843 Homeseekers begin gathering annually in the spring near the Missouri River bend to set out west toward the Oregon country. The trail they follow becomes known as the Oregon Trail.

1845 The phrase "manifest destiny" is used for perhaps the first time in reference to the United States' annexation of Texas.

1846–1848 The Mexican-American War occurs. The peace treaty gives the United States more than 500,000 square miles (1,300,000 square kilometers) of Mexican territory in the Southwest.

1850 California joins the Union as a free state under the terms of the Compromise of 1850.

1854 Congress passes the Kansas-Nebraska Act, enabling the people of those territories to vote on whether the territory would allow slavery.

GLOSSARY

acquisition The act of coming to own something.

annexation The incorporation of a country or other territory within the domain of a state.

cede To yield or grant control of something to another government, typically by treaty.

Continental Divide A ridge of north-south mountain summits that crosses western North America and separates the water flow on the continent.

emigrant A person who leaves a country or region to live in another one.

expansionism The belief that a country should grow larger; a policy of increasing a country's size by expanding its territory.

Federalist A member of the Federalist Party, which in the early years of the United States was in favor of a strong federal government. The Federalists held power from 1789 to 1801, during the rise of the country's political party system.

frontier A region that forms the margin of settled or developed territory.

grievance A cause of distress felt to afford reason for complaint or resistance.

Manifest Destiny In U.S. history, the supposed inevitability of the continued territorial expansion of the boundaries of the United States westward to the Pacific and beyond.

Protestant A Christian not of the Catholic or an Eastern Orthodox church.

right of deposit The right to store goods temporarily in advance of shipment.

strict constructionist One who favors a strict construction or interpretation of the U.S. Constitution.

Buffalo Bill Center of the West
720 Sheridan Avenue
Cody, Wyoming 82414
(307) 587-4771
Website: http://centerofthewest.org
The Buffalo Bill Center of the West hosts five museums
   that seek to share the story of the American West
   with new generations of young Americans.

Frontier Culture Museum
P.O. Box 810
1290 Richmond Road
Staunton, VA 24401
(540) 332-7850
Website: http://www.frontiermuseum.org
The Frontier Culture Museum gives visitors the chance
   to see how the earliest generations of American pioneers lived on the frontier.

Lewis and Clark Boat House and Nature Center
Bishop's Landing
1050 S. Riverside Drive
St. Charles, MO 63301
(636) 947-3199
Website: http://www.lewisandclarkcenter.org
The Lewis and Clark Boat House and Nature
   Center provides educational tours and houses a

museum dedicated to the historic Lewis and Clark Expedition.

Louisiana State Museum
P.O. Box 2448
New Orleans, LA 70176
(504) 568-6968
(800) 568-6968
Website: http://louisianastatemuseum.org
The Louisiana State Museum is a statewide network of museums and landmarks that document Louisiana's history and culture.

The National Museum of American History
14th Street & Constitution Avenue, NW
Washington, D.C. 20001
(202) 633-1000
Website: http://americanhistory.si.edu
The National Museum of American History preserves more than three million artifacts related to the history of the United States. Its exhibitions explore major episodes and themes of American history and culture.

State Historical Society of North Dakota
612 East Boulevard Avenue
Bismarck, ND 58505
(701) 328-2666
Website: http://history.nd.gov/exhibits/lewisclark/index.html

The State Historical Society of North Dakota's online Lewis and Clark exhibit provides an in-depth look at the historic expedition of 1804–06.

WEBSITES

Because of the changing nature of Internet links, Rosen Publishing has developed an online list of websites related to the subject of this book. This site is updated regularly. Please use this link to access the list:

http://www.rosenlinks.com/EAH/West

Benoit, Peter. *The Louisiana Purchase*. New York, NY: Children's Press, 2012.

Isserman, Maurice. *Across America: The Lewis and Clark Expedition*, rev. ed. New York, NY: Chelsea House, 2010.

Lanier, Wendy. *What Was the Missouri Compromise? And Other Questions About the Struggle over Slavery*. Minneapolis, MN: Lerner Publications, 2012.

Lewis, Meriwether, & William Clark. Gary E. Moulton, ed. *The Journals of the Lewis and Clark Expedition*. Lincoln, NE: University of Nebraska Press, 1983.

Robinson, Kate. *Lewis and Clark: Exploring the American West*. Berkeley Heights, NJ: Enslow Publishers, 2010.

Roza, Greg. *Westward Expansion*. New York, NY: Gareth Stevens Pub., 2011.

Sanford, William R., & Carl R. Green. *Sacagawea: Courageous American Indian Guide*. Berkeley Heights, NJ: Enslow Publishers, 2013.

Sanford, William R., & Carl R. Green. *Zebulon Pike: Courageous Rocky Mountain Explorer*. Berkeley Heights, NJ: Enslow Publishers, 2013.

Thompson, Linda. *Building an Empire: The Louisiana Purchase*. Vero Beach, FL: Rourke Educational Media, 2014.

INDEX

A

Algonquian, 17
American Revolution, 6, 22
Appalachian Mountains, 6, 25

B

Baton Rouge, 10, 22
Bienville, Jean-Baptiste Le
    Moyne, sieur de, 14, 16, 17
Biloxi, 14
Bonaparte, Napoleon, 23, 26, 28
Braddock, Edward, 21
Brazos River, 12
Brown, John, 67

C

California, 8, 59, 60, 61, 64, 65–66
Canada, 10, 11, 12, 22, 37
Charles IV, 23–24
Civil War, 67, 69
Clark, William, 7, 39–51
Columbia River, 8, 38, 41, 43, 45,
    56, 57
Compromise of 1850, 66
Continental Divide, 41, 43, 44, 57
Creoles, 16

D

Drouillard, George, 41

Duquesne, Fort, 21

E

England, 6, 17–22, 26, 28, 32, 34, 56

F

farming, 25, 26, 52, 56, 69
Far West, 38, 52–54
Florida, 22, 30, 32, 65
France
    exploration and rule of
        Louisiana, 10, 11–14, 17,
        25–26
    and the Far West, 53
    French and Indian War, 17–22
    Louisiana Purchase, 8–10,
        26–30
French and Indian War, 17–22
Frontenac, Fort, 12
Fugitive Slave Act, 67
fur trade, 10, 17, 38, 44, 54

G

Gray, Robert, 38
Great Lakes, 11
Green Bay, 12
Gulf of Mexico, 10, 11, 22

H

Harpers Ferry raid, 67